PIANO ✳ VOCAL ✳ GUITAR

HAPPY HOLIDAYS

ISBN 0-634-04918-6

HAL•LEONARD®
CORPORATION
777 W. BLUEMOUND RD. P.O. BOX 13819 MILWAUKEE, WI 53213

Visit Hal Leonard Online at
www.halleonard.com

BABY, IT'S COLD OUTSIDE

from the Motion Picture NEPTUNE'S DAUGHTER

By FRANK LOESSER

CHANUKAH

Words by SHELDON SECUNDA
Music by SHOLOM SECUNDA

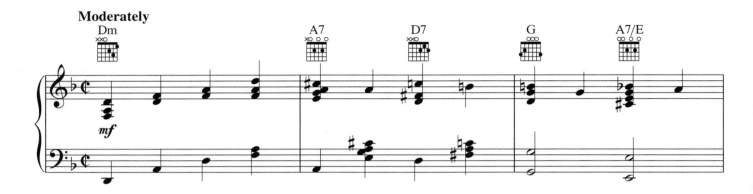

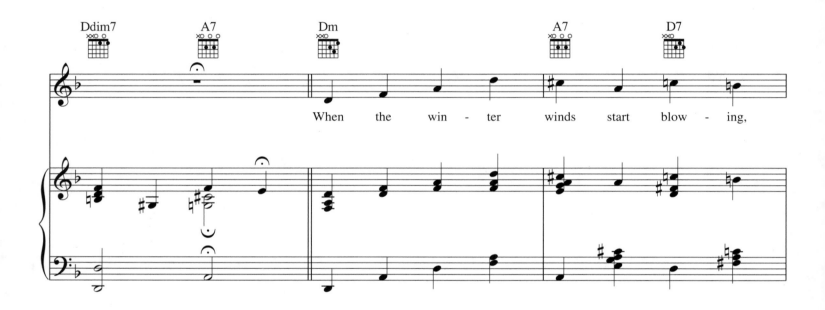

When the win - ter winds start blow - ing,

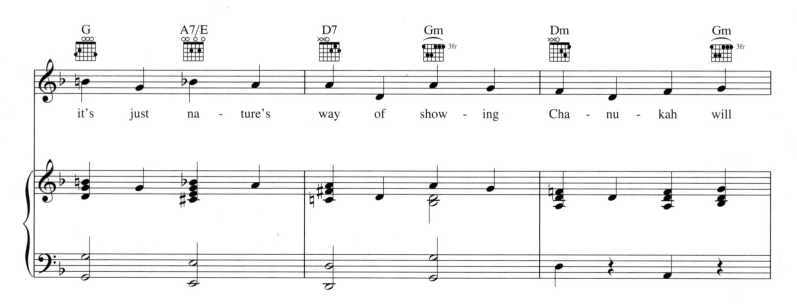

it's just na - ture's way of show - ing Cha - nu - kah will

CHRISTMAS BACK HOME

Words by LOONIS McGLOHON
Music by HUGH MARTIN

THE CHRISTMAS SONG
(Chestnuts Roasting on an Open Fire)

Music and Lyric by MEL TORME
and ROBERT WELLS

CHRISTMAS CHILD

Words and Music by
LOONIS McGLOHON

THE CHRISTMAS SHOES

Words and Music by LEONARD AHLSTROM
and EDDIE CARSWELL

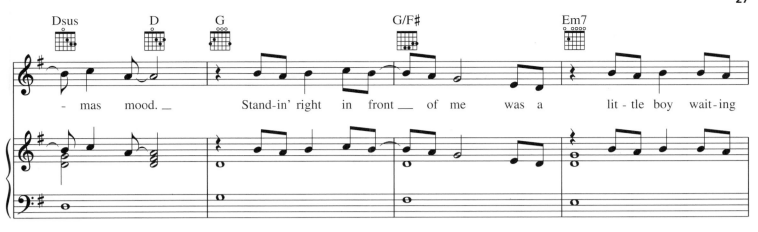

-mas mood. ___ Stand-in' right in front ___ of me was a lit-tle boy wait-ing

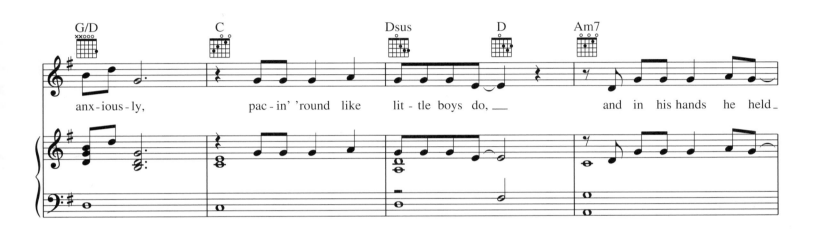

anx-ious-ly, pac-in' 'round like lit-tle boys do, ___ and in his hands he held ___

___ a pair of shoes. And his clothes were worn and old, ___

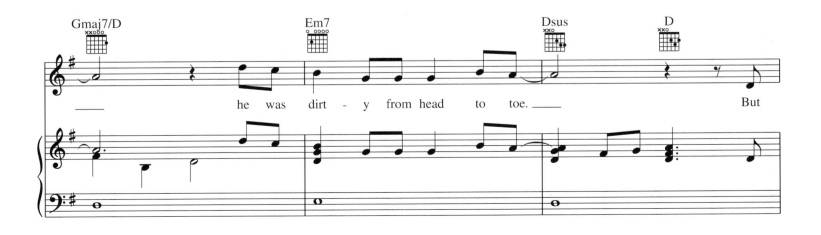

___ he was dirt-y from head to toe. ___ But

CHRISTMAS TIME IS HERE
from A CHARLIE BROWN CHRISTMAS

Words by LEE MENDELSON
Music by VINCE GUARALDI

Christ - mas time is here, hap - pi - ness and
Snow - flakes in the air, car - ols ev - 'ry -

cheer. Fun for all that chil - dren call their
where. Old - en times and an - cient rhymes their of

fa - v'rite time of year.
love and dreams to share.

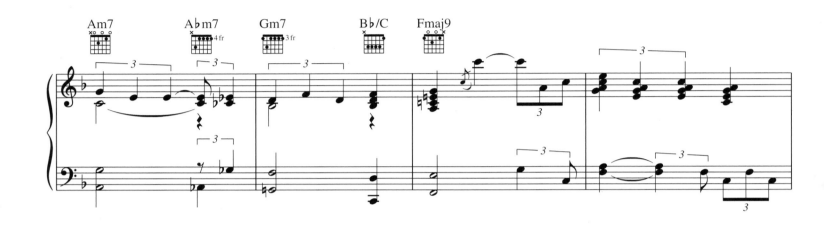

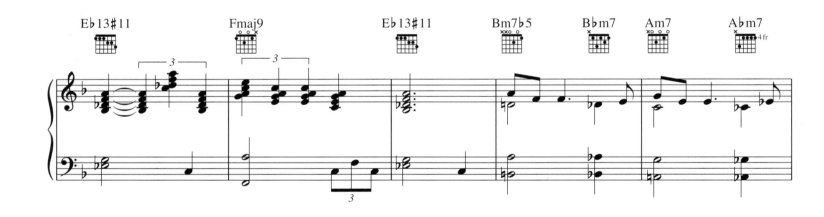

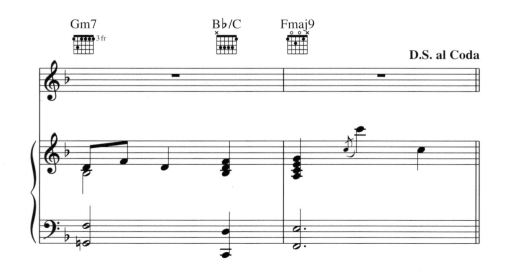

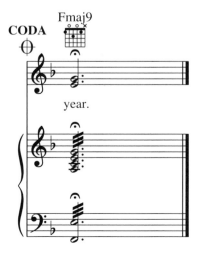

A DAY LIKE CHRISTMAS

Words and Music by MICHAEL S. BURNS
and LENORE ROSENBLATT

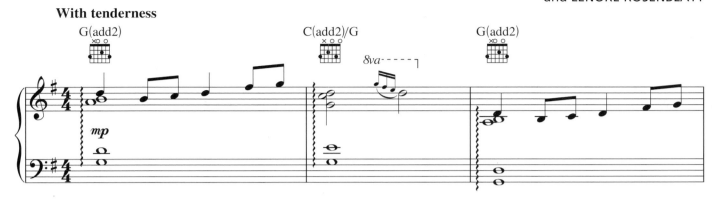

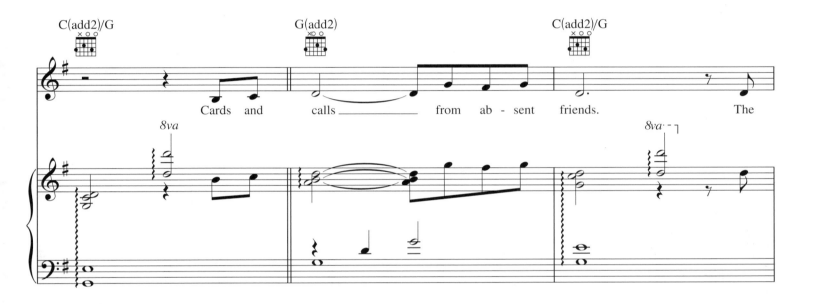

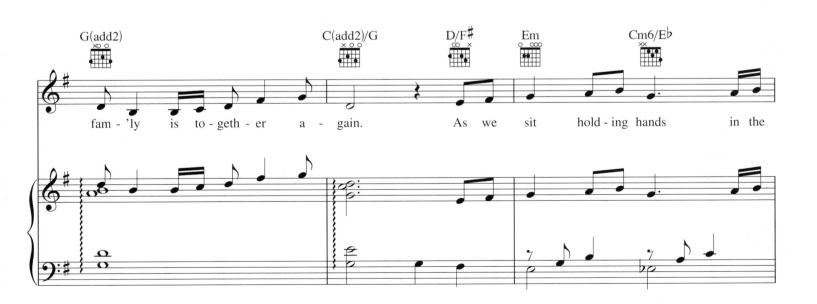

A CRADLE IN BETHLEHEM

Words and Music by AL BRYAN
and LAWRENCE STOCK

DO THEY KNOW IT'S CHRISTMAS?

Words and Music by M. URE
and B. GELDOF

DO YOU HEAR WHAT I HEAR

Words and Music by NOEL REGNEY
and GLORIA SHAYNE

EMMANUEL

Words and Music by
MICHAEL W. SMITH

FROSTY THE SNOW MAN

Words and Music by STEVE NELSON
and JACK ROLLINS

THE FIRST CHANUKAH NIGHT

Words by ENID FUTTERMAN
Music by MICHAEL COHEN

On the first Cha - nu - kah night we light one Cha - nu - kah

light in mem - 'ry of the mir - a - cle of the first Cha - nu - kah night. On the

sec - ond Cha - nu - kah night we light two Cha - nu - kah lights in

mem - 'ry of the mir - a - cle of the sec - ond Cha - nu - kah night.

On the

mp

A tempo

sev - enth Cha - nu - kah night we light sev - en Cha - nu - kah lights.

Is - n't it a mir - a - cle? Our sev - enth Cha - nu - kah night. On the

eighth Cha - nu - kah night we light eight Cha - nu - kah lights in

mem - 'ry of the mir - a - cle of the first Cha - nu - kah night.

FIRST DAY OF THE SON

Words and Music by
DERRICK PROCELL

The Son is here __ to stay. _____

Children: Christ - mas, Christ - mas, first day of __ the Son. __

Christ - mas, Christ - mas, sun - ny days for ev - 'ry - one. __

Male: Christ - mas, Christ - mas,
Children: (Christ - mas) (Christ - mas)

FOR THIS CHILD

Words and Music by
ROGER GILLEN

Left to my-self,___ I would be _____ a
Left to my-self,___ I would stand _____ a

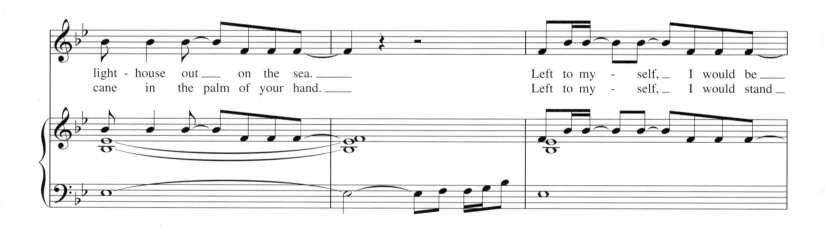

light-house out___ on the sea. _____
cane in the palm of your hand. _____

Left to my-self,___ I would be ____
Left to my-self,___ I would stand _

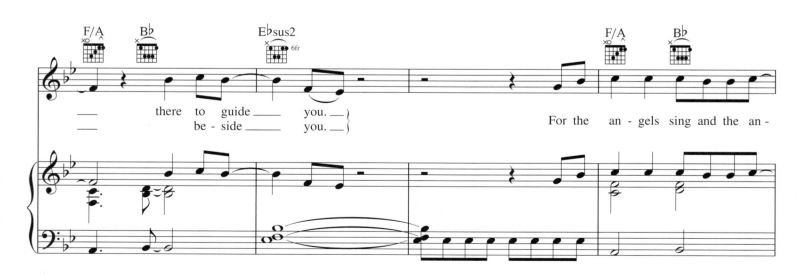

___ there to guide _____ you. ⎫
___ be-side _____ you. ⎭

For the an-gels sing and the an-

THE GIFT

Words and Music by TOM DOUGLAS
and JIM BRICKMAN

Slow Ballad

Female: Hoo.

Win-ter snow is fall-ing down, chil-dren laugh-ing all a-round,

lights are turn-ing on, like a fair-y tale come true.

GOD BLESS US EVERYONE

from A CHRISTMAS CAROL

Music by ALAN MENKEN
Lyrics by LYNN AHRENS

GROWN-UP CHRISTMAS LIST

Words and Music by DAVID FOSTER
and LINDA THOMPSON-JENNER

HAPPY HANUKKAH, MY FRIEND
(The Hanukkah Song)

Words and Music by DOUGLAS ALAN KONECKY
and JUSTIN WILDE

Spin the drei - del, light the lights,
Can - dle - light or Star A - bove,

HAPPY CHRISTMAS, LITTLE FRIEND

Lyrics by OSCAR HAMMERSTEIN II
Music by RICHARD RODGERS

HAPPY HOLIDAY

from the Motion Picture Irving Berlin's HOLIDAY INN

Words and Music by
IRVING BERLIN

HOLLY LEAVES AND CHRISTMAS TREES

Words and Music by RED WEST
and GLEN SPREEN

HAPPY XMAS
(War Is Over)

Words and Music by JOHN LENNON
and YOKO ONO

THE HOLIDAY SEASON

Words and Music by
KAY THOMPSON

I WONDER AS I WANDER

By JOHN JACOB NILES

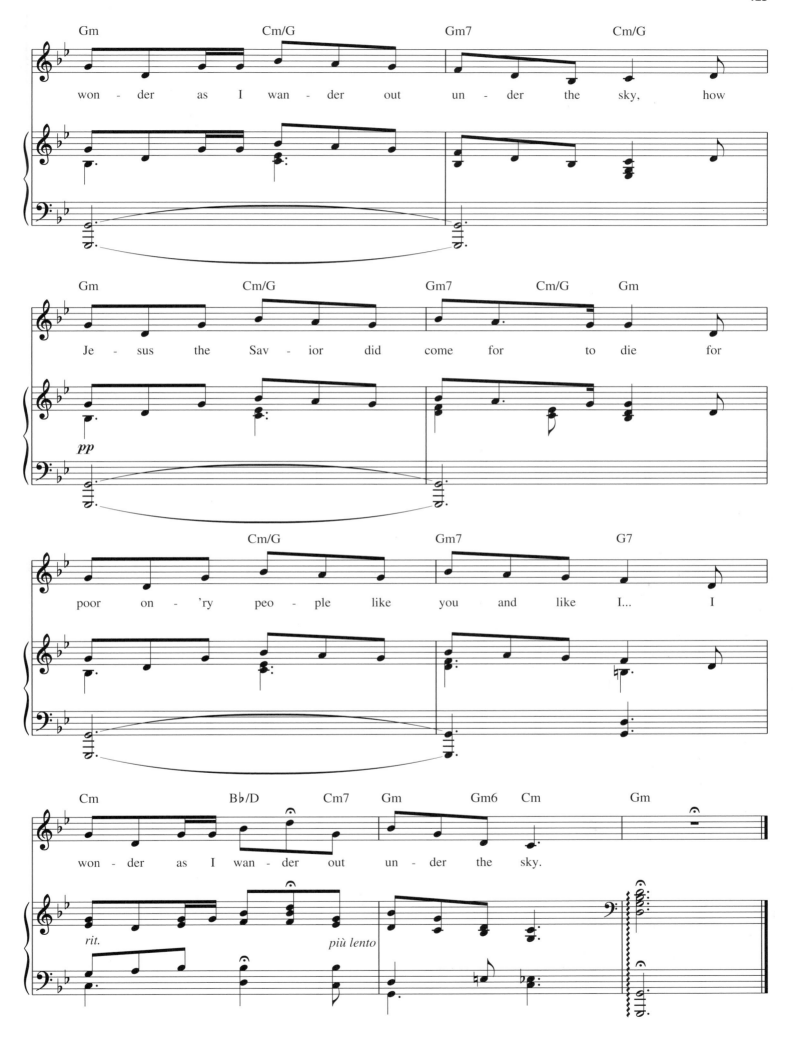

I YUST GO NUTS AT CHRISTMAS

Words and Music by
HARRY STEWART

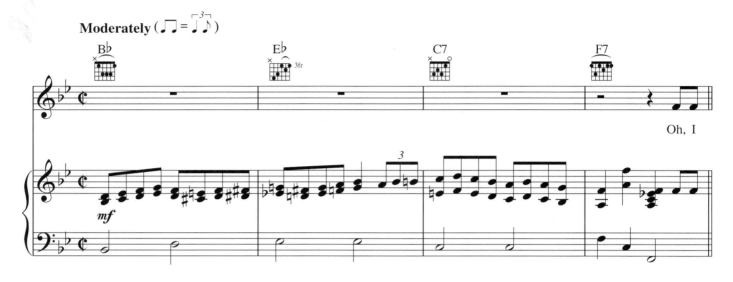

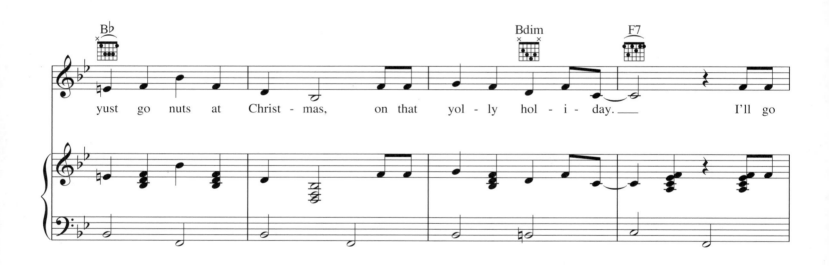

yust go nuts at Christ - mas when each kid hangs up his sock. It's a

time for kids to flip their lids while their pa - pa goes in hock.

Freely

(Spoken:) On the night before Christmas, it's still in the house. *My family is sleeping, so I'm quiet like a mouse.*

I look at my watch and midnight is near. I think I'll sneak out for a cold glass of beer.   Down at the corner the

crowd is so merry,   I end up by drinking about twelve Tom and Yerry.   I get to bed late and, gee

vhiz, how I'm sleeping,   when onto my bed those darn kids they come leaping.   They sit on my face and they yump on my

belly. And I'm quivering all over   They scream, "Merry Christmas!" My poor wife and me, we stumble downstairs and she
like a bowl full of yelly.

I'D LIKE TO GO
BACK HOME FOR CHRISTMAS

Words and Music by
LOONIS McGLOHON

I'LL BE HOME FOR CHRISTMAS

Words and Music by KIM GANNON
and WALTER KENT

IF I GET HOME ON CHRISTMAS DAY

Words and Music by
TONY MacAULEY

IT MUST HAVE BEEN THE MISTLETOE
(Our First Christmas)

By JUSTIN WILDE
and DOUG KONECKY

JINGLE, JINGLE, JINGLE

Music and Lyrics by
JOHNNY MARKS

Moderately, Gaily

THE LAST MONTH OF THE YEAR
(What Month Was Jesus Born In?)

Words and Music by
VERA HALL

MERRY CHRISTMAS, DARLING

Words and Music by RICHARD CARPENTER
and FRANK POOLER

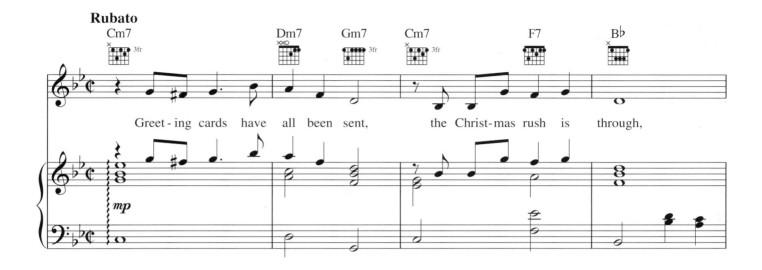

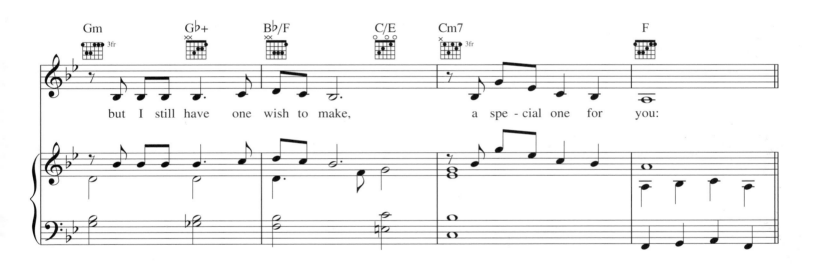

LITTLE SAINT NICK

Words and Music by BRIAN WILSON
and MIKE LOVE

Original key: G♭ major. This edition has been transposed up one half-step to be more playable.

A MERRY CHRISTMAS TO ME

Words and Music by DAN RODOWICZ
and PHILLIP KEVEREN

Warmly, with rubato

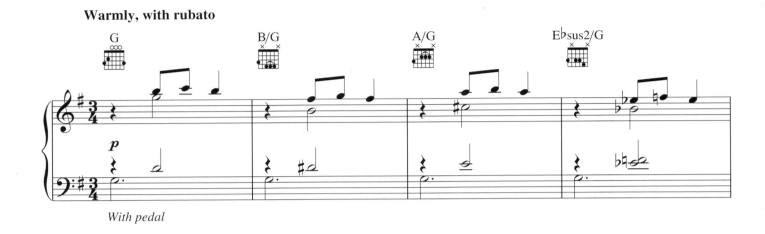

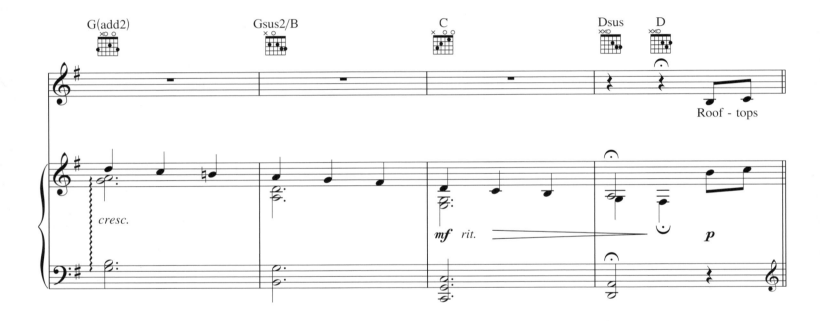

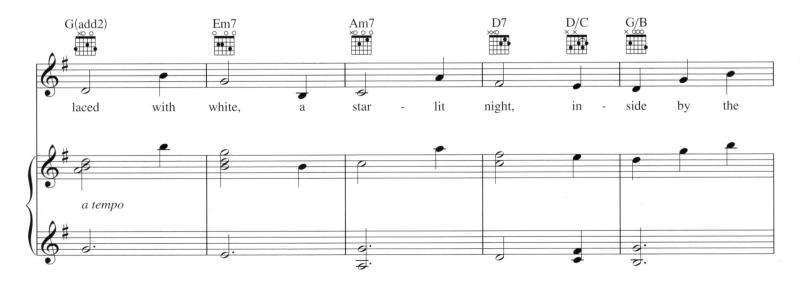

Rubato

G13 G7♭9 Cmaj7

But what I long to see won't be

A/B B7♭9 Em Em(maj7)

un - der my tree, though my wish is most sin -

G/A A9 G(add2)/D G(add2)/F

cere: _____ If the spir - it of Christ - mas would fill ev - 'ry

p *a tempo* *cresc. poco a poco*

Em7 Cm6/E♭

one of us and light each day of the year, _____ this would

f *mp*

THE MOST WONDERFUL TIME OF THE YEAR

Words and Music by EDDIE POLA
and GEORGE WYLE

CODA

C#m7   F#m7   E7sus/B   E7sus

most   won - der - ful   time   of the

Dm7   G7   Cmaj7   Am7   Dm7

year. _____

G7   Cmaj7   Cm7   F7

Bbmaj7   Ebmaj7   Cm   Am7b5   D7sus

NO MORE BLUE CHRISTMASES

Words and Music by GERRY GOFFIN
and MICHAEL MASSER

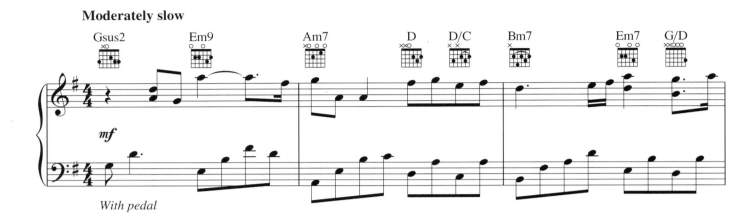

Oh, _____ no won-der that I thought that they were

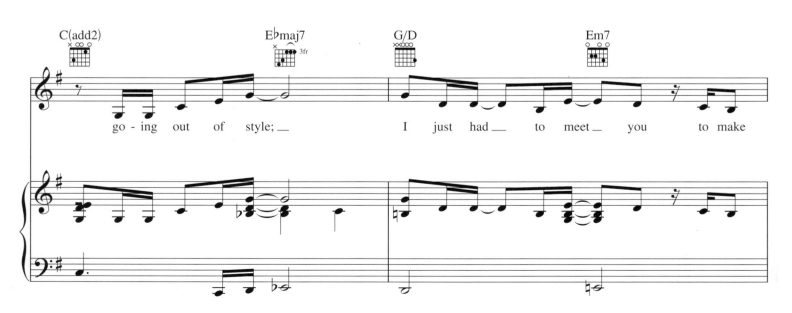

go-ing out of style; __ I just had __ to meet __ you to make

ONE GOD

Words and Music by ERVIN M. DRAKE
and JAMES SHIRL

A PLACE CALLED HOME
from A CHRISTMAS CAROL

Music by ALAN MENKEN
Lyrics by LYNN AHRENS

ROCKIN' AROUND THE CHRISTMAS TREE

Music and Lyrics by
JOHNNY MARKS

boughs of hol - ly." Rock - in' a - round the Christ - mas tree, ___ have a

hap - py hol - i - day. ___ Ev - 'ry - one danc - ing mer - ri - ly ___ in the

new old fash - ioned way.   new old fash - ioned

way. ___

SANTA CLAUS IS COMIN' TO TOWN

Words by HAVEN GILLESPIE
Music by J. FRED COOTS

RUDOLPH THE RED-NOSED REINDEER

Music and Lyrics by
JOHNNY MARKS

SILVER BELLS

from the Paramount Picture THE LEMON DROP KID

Words and Music by JAY LIVINGSTON
and RAY EVANS

THE STAR CAROL

Lyric by WIHLA HUTSON
Music by ALFRED BURT

WHAT ARE YOU DOING NEW YEAR'S EVE?

By FRANK LOESSER

WHEN A CHILD IS BORN

English Lyrics by FRED JAY
Music by ZACAR

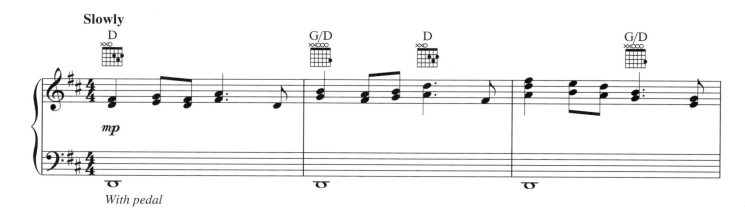

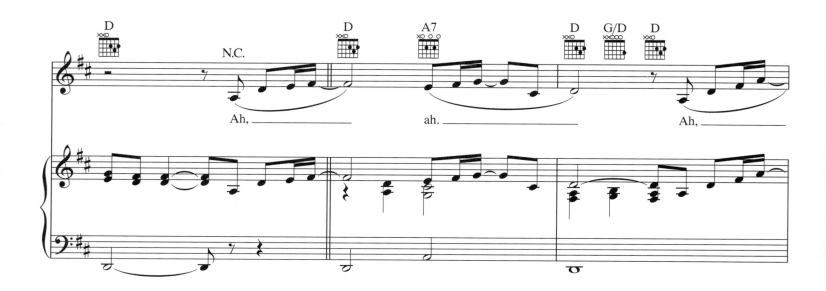

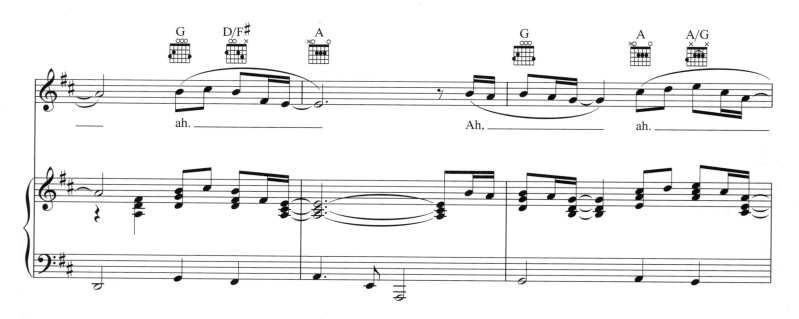

WHERE ARE YOU CHRISTMAS?

from DR. SEUSS' HOW THE GRINCH STOLE CHRISTMAS

Words and Music by WILL JENNINGS,
JAMES HORNER and MARIAH CAREY

Lyrics:
Where are you, Christ - mas? Why can't I find you? Why have you gone a-

WHO WOULD IMAGINE A KING

from the Touchstone Motion Picture THE PREACHER'S WIFE

Words and Music by MERVYN WARREN
and HALLERIN HILTON HILL

Gentle Waltz

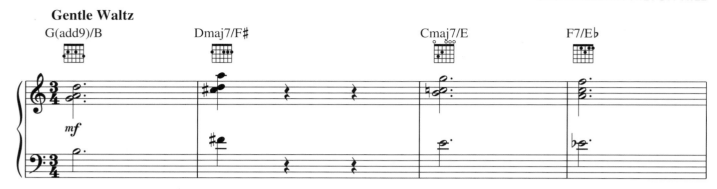

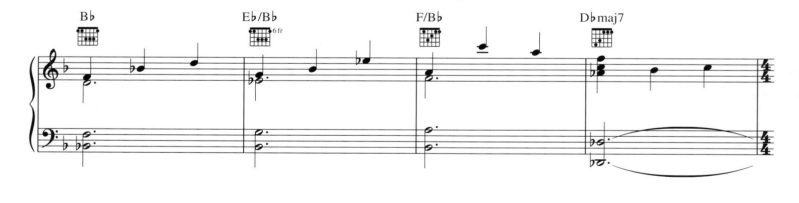

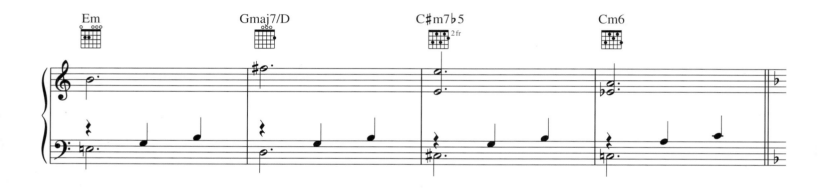

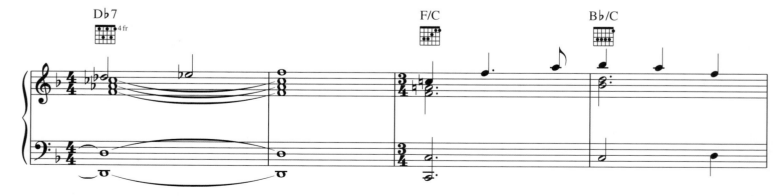

WONDERFUL CHRISTMASTIME

Words and Music by
McCARTNEY

Christmas Collections
From Hal Leonard
All books arranged for piano, voice, & guitar.

Christmas Time Is Here

A 50-song Christmas collection! Includes: As Long as There's Christmas • Caroling, Caroling • The Christmas Song • Christmas Time Is Here • Do You Hear What I Hear • Emmanuel • Feliz Navidad • Let's Make It Christmas All Year 'Round • The Most Wonderful Time of the Year • Santa Baby • Silver Bells • and more!

00311531 ....$16.95

The Best Christmas Songs Ever - 3rd Edition

A collection of more than 70 of the best-loved songs of the season, including: Blue Christmas • Frosty the Snow Man • Grandma Got Run Over by a Reindeer • I'll Be Home for Christmas • Jingle-Bell Rock • Rudolph, The Red-Nosed Reindeer • Silver Bells • You're All I Want for Christmas • and many more.

00359130 ....$19.95

The Big Book Of Christmas Songs

An outstanding collection of over 120 all-time Christmas favorites and hard-to-find classics. Features: Angels We Have Heard on High • As Each Happy Christmas • Auld Lang Syne • The Boar's Head Carol • Christ Was Born on Christmas Day • Bring a Torch Jeannette, Isabella • Carol of the Bells • Coventry Carol • Deck the Halls • The First Noel • The Friendly Beasts • God Rest Ye Merry Gentlemen • I Heard the Bells on Christmas Day • It Came Upon a Midnight Clear • Jesu, Joy of Man's Desiring • Joy to the World • Masters in This Hall • O Holy Night • The Story of the Shepherd • 'Twas the Night Before Christmas • What Child Is This? • and many more. Includes guitar chord frames.

00311520 ....$19.95

Season's Greetings

A great big collection of 50 favorites, including: All I Want for Christmas Is You • Blue Christmas • The Christmas Song • Frosty the Snow Man • Grandma Got Run Over by a Reindeer • Happy Holiday • I'll Be Home for Christmas • Most of All I Wish You Were Here • Silver Bells • What Made the Baby Cry? • and more.

00310426 ....$16.95

Christmas Songs For Kids

27 songs kids love to play during the holidays, including: Away in a Manger • The Chipmunk Song • Deck the Hall • The First Noel • Jingle Bells • Joy to the World • O Christmas Tree • Silent Night • and more.

00311571 ....$7.95

Contemporary Christian Christmas

20 songs as recorded by today's top Christian artists, including: Michael W. Smith (All Is Well) • Sandi Patty (Bethlehem Morning) • Amy Grant (Breath of Heaven) • Michael Card (Celebrate the Child) • Steven Curtis Chapman (Going Home for Christmas) • Michael English (Mary Did You Know?) • Steve Green (Rose of Bethlehem) • 4Him (A Strange Way to Save the World) • Point of Grace (This Gift) • Scott Wesley Brown (This Little Child) • and more.

00310643 ....$12.95

The Definitive Christmas Collection – 2nd Edition

All the Christmas songs you need in one convenient collection! Over 120 classics in all! Songs include: An Old Fashioned Christmas • Away in a Manger • The Chipmunk Song • Christmas Time Is Here • The Christmas Waltz • Do They Know It's Christmas • Feliz Navidad • The First Noel • Frosty the Snow Man • The Greatest Gift of All • Happy Holiday • A Holly Jolly Christmas • I Saw Mommy Kissing Santa Claus • Jingle-Bell Rock • Mister Santa • My Favorite Things • O Holy Night • Rudolph, The Red-Nosed Reindeer • Santa, Bring My Baby Back (To Me) • Silent Night • Silver Bells • Suzy Snowflake • We Need a Little Christmas • and many more.

00311602 ....$29.95

The Lighter Side of Christmas

42 fun festive favorites, including: Grandma Got Run Over by a Reindeer • A Holly Jolly Christmas • I Guess There Ain't No Santa Claus • I Saw Mommy Kissing Santa Claus • Jingle-Bell Rock • The Merry Christmas Polka • Rockin' Around the Christmas Tree • Rudolph the Red-Nosed Reindeer • That's What I'd Like for Christmas • and more.

00310628 ....$14.95

Ultimate Christmas - 3rd Edition

100 seasonal favorites, including: Auld Lang Syne • Bring a Torch, Jeannette, Isabella • Carol of the Bells • The Chipmunk Song • Christmas Time Is Here • The First Noel • Frosty the Snow Man • Gesù Bambino • Happy Holiday • Happy Xmas (War Is Over) • Hymne • Jesu, Joy of Man's Desiring • Jingle-Bell Rock • March of the Toys • My Favorite Things • The Night Before Christmas Song • Pretty Paper • Silver and Gold • Silver Bells • Suzy Snowflake • What Child Is This • The Wonderful World of Christmas • and more.

00361399 ....$19.95

FOR MORE INFORMATION, SEE YOUR LOCAL MUSIC DEALER,
OR WRITE TO:

HAL•LEONARD®
CORPORATION

7777 W. BLUEMOUND RD. P.O. BOX 13819 MILWAUKEE, WI 53213
http://www.halleonard.com

PRICES, CONTENTS, AND AVAILABILITY SUBJECT TO CHANGE WITHOUT NOTICE.

0802